Cooking the

Mongolian Way!

Delicious Recipes from The Mongolian

Cuisine!

BY: Valeria Ray

License Notes

Table of Contents

Introduction

Mongolian food is pretty big on flavor! The cuisine takes inspiration from surrounding Asian countries such as China. If one word describes a Moroccan dining table, it would probably be "soul food". Meals in Mongolia are generally a very social occasion with large families sitting down together to share a meal!

Whether you enjoy lighter healthier food or are in the mood for a more flavorsome feast, there's something for everyone at a Mongolian meal!

1. Traditional Mongolian Beef

Crunchy sticky beef, this recipe is a Mongolian classic waiting to be devoured!

Prep Time: 10 mins

Total Time: 30 mins

Servings: 2

Ingredients

- 2 tsp vegetable oil
- 1 lb. flank steak
- 1/2 tsp ginger, minced
- 1/4 C. cornstarch
- 1 tbsp. garlic, chopped
- 2 large green onions, sliced thin
- 1/2 C. soy sauce
- into one-inch lengths
- 1/2 C. water
- 3/4 C. dark brown sugar
- Vegetable oil, for frying (about 1 C.)

Directions

1. For the sauce: in a medium pan, heat 2 tsp of the vegetable oil on medium-low heat and sauté the ginger and garlic with the soy sauce a little.

2. Then, stir in the water.

3. Add in brown sugar and mix till sugar is dissolved.

4. Increase the heat to medium and cook for about 2-3 minutes, stirring continuously.

5. Remove from the heat.

6. Cut steak into 1/4-inch thick bite-size slices.

7. Coat the steak slices with the cornstarch slightly and keep aside for about 10 minutes.

8. In a wok, heat 1 C. of the oil on medium heat and sear the beef slices for about 2 minutes.

9. With a slotted spoon, transfer the beef onto paper towels lined plate to drain.

10. Remove the oil from the wok.

11. Return the beef in pan on heat and simmer for about 1 minute.

12. Stir in the sauce and cook for about 1 minute, stirring continuously.

13. Add in green onions and cook for about 1 minute, stirring continuously.

14. Serve warm over rice!

2. Lamb from Mongolia

These easy 30 minutes recipe is perfect for a quick and easy, but delicious dinner!

Prep Time: 15 mins

Total Time: 30 mins

Servings per recipe: 4

Ingredients

- 2.5 tbsp. oil
- 2.5 tbsp. sweet chili sauce
- 1 lb. lamb fillets, cut into thin strips
- 2 tsp toasted sesame seeds
- 2 cloves garlic, crushed
- 4 spring onions
- 2. 5 tbsp. soy sauce
- 5 tbsp. dry sherry

Directions

1. In a wok, heat half the oil and stir fry the lamb in batches for about 3 minutes.

2. Transfer the lamb into a bowl.

3. In the same wok, using the rest of the oil, sauté the garlic and spring onion for about 2 minutes.

4. Transfer the garlic mixture into a small bowl.

5. In the same wok, add the sherry and sauces and bring to a boil.

6. Reduce the heat and simmer for about 3-4 minutes.

7. Stir in the lamb and garlic mixture and cook till heated through and toss to coat with the sauce.

8. Serve with a sprinkling of the sesame seeds.

3. Thursday's 30-Minute Beef

This recipes is a quicker version of the classic Mongolian beef but just as delicious!

Prep Time: 15 mins

Total Time: 30 mins

Servings per recipe: 2

Ingredients

- 10 oz. beef, sliced into 3/8-inch strips
- 2/3 C. sugar
- 1/4 C. cornstarch
- 1/4 yellow onion, sliced
- 4 C. vegetable oil
- 2 green onions, sliced
- 2 tsp vegetable oil
- 1/4 tsp white pepper
- 1/2 tsp chopped garlic
- 1/4 tsp sesame seed oil
- 1 tsp rice wine vinegar
- 1/4 C. soy sauce

Directions

1. Coat the beef with the cornstarch and keep aside for about 5 minutes.

2. In a deep skillet, heat 4 C. of the vegetable oil and fry beef till crispy.

3. Transfer the beef onto a plate.

4. In another skillet, heat 2 tsp of the vegetable oil and sauté the garlic, rice wine, soy sauce and beef well.

5. Stir in the sugar and stir fry for about 1 minute.

6. Stir in the yellow onion, green onion and white pepper and stir well.

7. Stir in the sesame oil and serve.

4. Beef Bok Choy

Looking to get in more greens into your meals? This beef bok choy recipe is the perfect way to do it!

Prep Time: 10 mins

Total Time: 15 mins

Servings per recipe: 4

Ingredients

- 1 tbsp. oyster sauce
- 3 C. flank steaks, sliced thinly against the grain
- 2 cloves finely chopped garlic
- 1/2 C. vegetable oil, divided
- 1/2 tbsp. sesame oil
- 1 C. shiitake mushroom, thinly sliced
- 1/4 C. light soy sauce
- 1 C. bok choy
- 1/3 C. chicken broth
- 1 tbsp. oyster sauce
- 1/8 C. fresh ginger

Directions

1. In a bowl, mix together the steak, 1/4 veggie oil, and oyster sauce.

2. Using a different bowl, combine the broth and sesame oil.

3. In a hot wok, heat the remaining vegetable oil and sauté the garlic and ginger till aromatic.

4. Add the flank steak and sauté for about 2 minutes.

5. Add the mushroom and bok choy and sauté for about 2 minutes.

6. Add the soy sauce and cook for about 30 seconds.

5. Mongolian Dump Dinner

Leave this in a crockpot before you head to work and return home to a delicious dinner!

Prep Time: 10 mins

Total Time: 8 hr 10 mins

Servings per recipe: 4

Ingredients

- 1 1/2-2 lb. London broil beef (cut in to strips)
- 3 -4 large carrots, thickly sliced
- 2 garlic cloves, minced
- 3/4 C. soy sauce
- 1/4 C. cornstarch
- 1/2 C. water
- 1 medium onion, thinly sliced
- 1/4 C. broth
- 3/4 C. brown sugar
- 1/2 tsp ginger, minced
- 1/4 tsp black pepper

Directions

1. Coat the beef strips with the cornstarch and keep aside.

2. In a crock pot, add the remaining Ingredients and mix well.

3. Place beef strips over the mixture.

4. Leave the crock pot on low and cook, covered for about 6-8 hours. Serve warm!

6. Wontons

This recipe makes crispy, crunchy and delicious beef wontons!

Prep Time: 15 mins

Total Time: 25 mins

Servings per recipe: 2

Ingredients

- 8 wonton wrappers
- Sea salt and pepper
- 1/2 lb. ground lamb
- 1 C. Greek yogurt, placed in a cheesecloth-lined sieve (drained overnight in the fridge)
- 1/3 C. onion, minced
- 1 tsp garlic, minced
- 2 tbsp. fresh parsley, minced
- 4 tsp dried mint
- 1 jalapeño pepper, minced

Directions

1. In a bowl, add the lamb, onion, garlic, parsley, jalapeño pepper, salt and black pepper and mix well.

2. Refrigerate to chill completely.

3. Arrange the wrapper onto a smooth surface.

4. Place a tsp of the lamb mixture over each wrapper and fold to form a half circle, sealing with wet fingers.

5. Arrange the dumplings onto baking sheet dusted with the cornstarch.

6. In a pan of the rapidly boiling salted water, add the dumplings and stir once.

7. Cook for about 2 minutes.

8. Transfer onto a paper towels lined plate to drain.

9. In a large sauté pan, add yogurt on medium heat and cook till warmed.

10. Add the hot dumplings and toss to coat well.

11. Divide the dumpling mixture into serving bowls and serve with a sprinkling of the dried mint.

7. Beef and Asparagus

Another Mongolian classic, this beef and asparagus uses traditional Mongolian flavours and is absolutely delicious!

Prep Time: 1 hr 20 mins

Total Time: 1 hr 35 mins

Servings per recipe: 4

Ingredients

- 1 lb. flank steak
- 4 tbsp. peanut oil
- 2 tbsp. light soy sauce
- 1 clove garlic, minced
- 3 tbsp. hoisin sauce
- 1 slice fresh ginger, minced
- 1 tbsp. rice wine
- 1/8 tsp crushed red pepper flakes
- 1 tbsp. cornstarch
- 1 tsp sugar
- 1 1/2 lb. asparagus

Directions

1. Slice steak thinly and then, cut into 2-inch wide strips.

2. In a bowl, add the hoisin, soy, cornstarch, rice wine, and sugar and mix well.

3. Add steak strips and coat with marinade generously.

4. Refrigerate to marinate for about 1 hour.

5. In a pan of the boiling water, blanch the asparagus for about 5 minutes.

6. In a skillet, heat 2 tbsp. of the oil and stir fry the asparagus for about 2 minutes.

7. Transfer the asparagus into a bowl.

8. Further heat 2 tbsp. oil and sauté the ginger, garlic and red pepper flakes for about 1 minute.

9. Add in beef and stir fry for about 3-4 minutes. Serve!

8. 10 Ingredient Mongolian Dinner

On a budget? This simple 10 ingredient recipe is perfect if you're looking to simplify things

Prep Time: 4 hr

Total Time: 4 hr

Servings per recipe: 4

Ingredients

- 1 lb. flank steak
- 1/2 C. water
- 1/4 C. cornstarch
- 3/4 C. brown sugar
- 2 tsp olive oil
- 2 large green onions, chopped
- 1/2 tsp minced ginger
- 1 C. cooked basmati rice
- 1 tbsp. minced garlic
- 1/2 C. soy sauce

Directions

1. Cut steak into bite size pieces and coat with the cornstarch evenly.

2. Keep aside for about 10 minutes.

3. In a skillet, heat the oil and sear for about 2-4 minutes.

4. Transfer the beef into a crock pot.

5. Add remaining **Ingredients** and mix well.

6. Set crock pot on low. Keep covered and cook for about 4 hours.

7. Enjoy with rice topped liberally with sauce from the crock pot.

9. Teriyaki Salmon

Wow guests with this easy but elegant dinner meal!

Prep Time: 8 hr

Total Time: 8 hr 12 mins

Servings per recipe: 4

Ingredients

- 1 lb. salmon fillet
- 1 C. teriyaki sauce or 1 C. teriyaki marinade
- 1/4 C. honey

Directions

1. Get a large bag: Place it in the salmon fillets with teriyaki sauce. Seal the bag and shake it to coat.

2. Before you do anything preheat the grill and grease it.

3. Remove the salmon fillets from the marinade. Cook it on the grill with skin side facing up for 4 min.

4. Rotate the fillet on the other side and cook it for another 4 min. Flip the salmon fillet and brush it with honey. Cook it for 7 min then serve it warm.

5. Enjoy

10. Ground Beef Salad

Make this yummy Mongolian Beef Lettuce wraps for a quick and easy lunch option!

Prep Time: 15 mins

Total Time: 40 mins

Servings per recipe: 4

Ingredients

- 4 C. lettuce, coarsely torn
- 1/2 C. warm water
- 1 tbsp. ginger, minced
- 2 tsp cornstarch
- 1 tbsp. garlic, minced
- 1 tbsp. cold water
- 1/2 lb. ground beef
- 1/2 tsp toasted sesame oil
- 1/2 tsp salt
- 1 tbsp. soy sauce
- 1 tbsp. rice vinegar

Directions

1. In a large skillet, heat oil on medium-high heat and sauté the garlic for about 10 seconds.

2. Add the ginger and sauté till slightly softened.

3. Add the meat and salt cook till browned, breaking the lumps.

4. Stir in the soy sauce, vinegar and warm water and bring to a boil.

5. Combine the cornstarch in the cold water.

6. Add the cornstarch mixture into skillet and stir to combine well.

7. Stir in the sesame oil and remove from the heat.

8. In a wide salad bowl, place the lettuce.

9. Immediately, pour the hot sauce and toss to coat.

10. Serve immediately.

11. Sweet Garlic Sriracha Steak

Sticky and sweet, these Sriracha glazed steaks are absolutely divine!

Prep Time: 30 mins

Total Time: 45 mins

Servings per recipe: 6

Ingredients

- 1/4 C. hoisin sauce
- 1 tbsp. chopped fresh ginger
- 1/4 C. low sodium chicken broth
- 1 tsp Sriracha sauce
- 2 tbsp. rice vinegar
- 1 1/2 lb. flank steaks
- 2 tbsp. chopped garlic
- 1/2 tsp salt
- 2 tbsp. toasted sesame oil
- 1/2 tsp black pepper
- 1 tbsp. brown sugar
- 1 tbsp. low sodium soy sauce

Directions

1. To a food processor, mix in the hoisin sauce, Sriracha, vinegar, broth, sesame oil, brown sugar, soy sauce, garlic and ginger and pulse till smooth.

2. Score a diamond pattern over one side of steak.

3. In a ziplock, add steak and sauce.

4. Seal the bag and shake to coat.

5. Keep aside in the room temperature for at least 20 minutes.

6. Set your grill to high and grease the grill grate.

7. Remove beef and season with the salt and pepper.

8. Arrange the steak onto grill and cook, covered for about 5 minutes.

9. Flip and cook till desired doneness.

10. Transfer the steak onto cutting board and keep aside for about 5 minutes before slicing

11. Cut steak against into thin slices and serve.

12. Kebabs

These kebabs take on delicious Mongolian flavours for a filling meal option!

Prep Time: 15 mins

Total Time: 30 mins

Servings per recipe: 1

Ingredients

- 2 1/2 lb. flank steaks
- 1/2 tsp sugar
- 1/2 C. hoisin sauce
- 1/2 tsp pepper
- 2 tbsp. peanut oil
- 1/2 tsp fresh ginger, grated
- 2 tbsp. sesame oil
- 1 garlic clove, crushed
- 2 tbsp. broth
- 2 tbsp. soy sauce

Directions

1. Cut the steak across grain into 1/8-inch thick strips diagonally.

2. In a large heavy-duty zip lock plastic bag, add the beef and remaining all Ingredients.

3. Seal the bag and shake to coat.

4. Refrigerator for 8 hours, flipping occasionally.

5. Meanwhile, soak the 32 (6-inch) wooden skewers in water for at least 10 minutes.

6. Set the broiler of your oven and arrange oven rack about 3-inch from the heating element.

7. Thread steak onto pre-soaked skewers.

8. Cook under the broiler for about 2-3 minutes per side.

13. Crock Pot Beef

Dump in all the **Ingredients** for a delicious but easy to prepare meal!

Prep Time: 10 mins

Total Time: 6 hr 10 mins

Servings per recipe: 2

Ingredients

- 1 1/2 lb. beef flank steak, sliced thinly
- 3/4 C. soy sauce
- 3/4 C. water
- 1/4 C. cornstarch
- 3/4 C. brown sugar
- 2 tbsp. olive oil
- 1/2 C. shredded carrot
- 1/2 tsp minced ginger
- 3 medium green onions, diced
- 2 garlic cloves, minced

Directions

1. Grease a slow cooker.

2. Coat each piece of steak with the cornstarch evenly and transfer into a crock pot.

3. Mix together rest of the Ingredients and mix well.

4. Place the mixture over beef.

5. Cook on high for about 2-3 hours. Serve warm!

14. Tasty Chicken Meatballs

Delicious and moist meatballs that are super simple to make!

Prep Time: 10 mins

Total Time: 35 mins

Servings per recipe: 6

Ingredients

- 1 lb. minced chicken
- 4 tbsp. teriyaki sauce
- 1/2 tsp grated gingerroot (optional)
- 2 green onions, sliced
- Garlic salt

Directions

1. Preheat oven to 350 F.

2. Get a large mixing bowl: Combine in it all the Ingredients. Mix them well. Shape the mix into 1 inch meatballs.

3. Place meatballs on a lined baking sheet. Cook them in the oven for 28 min. Serve them warm.

15. Spicy Pomegranate Marinade

Looking for a delicious marinade for your dinner protein? Try out this delicious pomegranate marinade!

Prep Time: 5 mins

Total Time: 20 mins

Marinade

Servings per recipe: 1

Ingredients

- 1 tsp chili powder
- 2 tbsp. dark soy sauce
- 2 tsp ground cumin
- 2 tbsp. olive oil
- 1/2 lemon, juiced
- 3 tbsp. pomegranate molasses

Directions

1. In a bowl, combine together all the Ingredients.

2. Add the lamb and coat with marinade generously.

3. Refrigerator overnight before cooking.

16. Mongolian Basmati with Tofu

This super easy recipe calls for tofu for all your vegan friends and family!

Prep Time: 10 mins

Total Time: 20 mins

Servings per recipe: 3

Ingredients

- 1/4 C. tamari
- 1/2 lb. firm tofu
- 1 tbsp. brown sugar
- 2 tbsp. peanut oil
- 1 tbsp. garlic, minced
- 1/2 medium yellow onion, chopped
- 1 tbsp. ginger, crushed
- 2 large carrots, sliced
- 1 tsp hoisin sauce
- 1 green onion
- 1 tbsp. sesame oil
- 1 C. basmati rice
- 1 tbsp. water
- 2 C. water

Directions

1. Chop the tofu in medium strips.

2. In a baking dish, mix together the tamari, brown sugar, garlic, ginger, Hoisin sauce, sesame oil and water.

3. Add the tofu and coat with the marinade generously.

4. Refrigerate, covered for about 1/2-1 hour.

5. Prepare the rice according to package's directions.

6. In a pan, heat peanut oil on medium heat and sauté the onion and carrots till onion is translucent.

7. Add the tofu and sauce and stir fry for about 5-10 minutes.

8. Serve alongside the rice with a topping of the chopped green onion.

17. Grilled Teriyaki Tuna

Delicious Tuna fillets are coated in an easy to prep teriyaki glaze!

Prep Time: 8 hr

Total Time: 8 hr 12 mins

Servings per recipe: 4

Ingredients

- 1 lb. Tuna fillets
- 1 C. teriyaki sauce or 1 C. teriyaki marinade
- 1/4 C. honey

Directions

1. Get a large bag: Place it in the salmon fillets with teriyaki sauce. Seal the bag and shake it to coat.

2. Before you do anything preheat the grill and grease it.

3. Remove the salmon fillets from the marinade. Cook it on the grill with skin side facing up for 4 min.

4. Rotate the fillet on the other side and cook it for another 4 min. Flip the salmon fillet and brush it with honey. Cook it for 7 min then serve it warm.

5. Enjoy

18. Marinade II

Here's another delicious marinade recipe for a quick dinner option!

Prep Time: 5 mins

Total Time: 10 mins

Servings per recipe: 4

Ingredients

- 1 tsp olive oil
- 1/2 tsp ginger powder
- 1 tbsp. minced garlic
- 1/2 C. soy sauce
- 1/2 C. water
- 1/4 C. brown sugar

Directions

1. In a wok, heat oil and sauté the ginger and garlic till aromatic.

2. Add the water, soy sauce and sugar and cook till sugar dissolves, stirring continuously.

3. Boil, then reduce the heat to low.

4. Simmer till the desired thickness of the sauce.

19. Lunch Box Salad

Looking for a healthy and easy to put together lunch option? Try out this delicious Mongolian salad recipe!

Prep Time: 30 mins

Total Time: 40 mins

Servings per recipe: 4

Ingredients

For Marinade:

- 1 C. fresh orange juice
- 1/4 C. grated orange zest
- 1/4 C. honey
- 2 tbsp. soy sauce
- 2 tsp chopped. Peeled fresh ginger
- 2 tsp minced garlic
- 1/4 tsp dried red pepper flakes
- 4 (3/4 lb.) boneless beef top loin steaks, fat trimmed

Dressing:

- 2 tbsp. red vinegar
- 1 tbsp. mustard
- 2 sprigs chopped fresh tarragon or 1 tsp dried tarragon, crumbled
- 1 tbsp. chopped shallots or 1 tbsp. green onion
- 1/2 tsp minced garlic
- 1/2 C. olive oil
- Assorted mixed greens, such as Boston lettuce, oak leaf lettuce, and mustard

Directions

1. For the marinade: in a large shallow glass baking dish, mix together all the Ingredients well.

2. Cover and keep aside in the room temperature for about 1 hour.

3. For the dressing: in a bowl, add the vinegar, mustard, tarragon, shallots, garlic, salt and pepper and beat till well combined.

4. Add the oil in slow steady stream and beat well. Season to taste with.

5. Set your barbecue to high heat.

6. Remove steaks from the baking dish, reserving the marinade.

7. Cook the steaks on grill for about 5 minutes per side, basting with the reserved marinade occasionally.

8. Remove from the grill and cut the steaks into thin slices.

9. In a large bowl, add the greens and enough dressing and toss to coat.

10. Divide greens onto serving plates and top with the steak slices, torn into bite-sized pieces.

11. Serve immediately with any extra dressing.

20. Heart of Mongolia Punch

This punch is super delicious and goes perfectly with the tropical Mongolian flavours

Prep Time: 10 mins

Total Time: 10 mins

Servings per recipe: 4

Ingredients

- 1 C. chopped fresh strawberries
- 1 C. orange juice
- 10 cubes ice
- 1 tbsp. sugar

Directions

1. In a blender, add all the Ingredients and pulse till smooth.

2. Transfer into glasses and serve immediately.

21. Potato Quarters

Crispy and delicious potato wedges coated in delicious
Mongolian **Ingredients**!

Prep Time: 10 mins

Total Time: 26 mins

Servings per recipe: 5

Ingredients

- 1 and a half lb. small sized skinned potatoes
- Pinch of Italian seasoning, crushed
- 1/8 tsp black pepper, to taste
- 1 tbsp. butter or 1 tbsp. margarine, cut into pieces
- 1/8 cayenne pepper, to taste
- 1 tsp fresh rosemary, minced (optional)
- 1 tbsp. bottled teriyaki sauce
- Sour cream, to garnish (optional)
- 1/4 tsp garlic salt, to taste

Directions

1. Clean the potatoes and slice them into quarters. Place it in a microwave proof pan.

2. Add to it the remaining Ingredients except for the rosemary and mix them. Put on the lid and microwave them for 17 min on high or until the potatoes becomes soft.

3. Stir in the rosemary then serve your potato casserole warm.

4. Enjoy.

22. Glazed Swordfish

This recipes uses the swordfish in the best way possible for a delicious meal!

Prep Time: 15 mins

Total Time: 3 hr 15 mins

Servings per recipe: 4

Ingredients

- 2 tbsp. canola oil
- 1/4 C. chopped white onion
- 2 -3 minced garlic cloves
- 1 1/2 tsp grated fresh ginger
- 1/2 C. teriyaki sauce
- 1/4 honey
- 4 (6 oz.) center cut swordfish steaks

Directions

1. Place a saucepan over medium heat. Heat the oil in it. Cook in it the onion, garlic and ginger for 4 min.

2. Stir in the honey with teriyaki sauce. Cook them until they start boiling while stirring all the time. Lower the heat and cook them for 3 min.

3. Place the sauce aside to lose heat. Reserve 1/4 of the sauce.

4. Get a large zip lock bag: Place in it the remaining sauce with swordfish steaks. Seal the bag and shake it to coat. Place it in the fridge for 2 h 30.

5. Before you do anything preheat the grill for 6 min and grease it.

6. Drain the swordfish from the sauce. Cook the swordfish steaks in the grill for 5 min on each side.

7. Remove the steaks from the grill and spray them with a cooking spray. Wipe the grill clean.

8. Cook the swordfish for 4 min on each side with basting them with the reserved sauce.

9. Serve your swordfish steaks warm.

10. Enjoy.

23. Teriyaki Meat

Try out this recipe with any protein of your choice –
poultry, red meat, or seafood, it's amazing any way!

Prep Time: 15 mins

Total Time: 25 mins

Servings per recipe: 10

Ingredients

- 3 -4 lb. meat of your choice
- 3 green onions (chopped fine)

Sauce:

- 1 tsp Chinese five spice powder (optional)
- 2/3 C. shoyu (Asian soy sauce)
- 1/2 C. sugar
- 2 tbsp. broth
- 3 garlic cloves, minced
- 1 inch piece ginger, crushed

Directions

1. Get a large zip lock bag: Combine in it all the Ingredients. Seal the bag and shake it to coat. Place it in the fridge for 5 h to an overnight.

2. Before you do anything preheat the oven to 325 F.

3. Pour the mix into a roasting casserole dish. Cook it in the oven for 1 h 10 min. Serve your meat casserole warm.

24. Tuna Steaks

This recipe takes the simple tuna steak to a whole new level!

Prep Time: 2 hr

Total Time: 2 hr 12 mins

Servings per recipe: 4

Ingredients

- 1/4 C. soy sauce
- 3 cloves garlic, minced
- 3 tbsp. brown sugar
- 1 tsp ground ginger
- 3 tbsp. olive oil
- 1/8 tsp black pepper
- 2 tbsp. white wine vinegar
- 4 tuna steaks (about 6 oz. each)
- 2 tbsp. chicken broth
- 2 tbsp. unsweetened pineapple juice

Directions

1. Get a large mixing bowl: Mix in it all the Ingredients except for the tuna steaks to make the marinade.

2. Get a large zip lock bag: Place in it the tuna steaks with marinade. Seal it and shake it to coat. Chill for 1 h 20 min.

3. Before you do anything preheat the grill and grease it.

4. Remove tuna steaks from the marinade and grill them for 7 min on each side while basting them with the marinade.

5. Serve your steaks warm.

25. Chicken Kebabs

Chicken version of the delicious Beef Mongolian Kebabs

Prep Time: 1 hr 30 mins

Total Time: 2 hr

Servings per recipe: 24

Ingredients

- 1 tbsp. sesame seeds, toasted
- 1 tbsp. Splenda granular (sugar substitute)
- 2 lbs. of boneless skinless chicken thighs

Marinade

- 6 tbsp. sesame oil
- 15 oz. of teriyaki sauce
- 1 lemon, juice of
- 1/4 tsp minced garlic

Directions

1. Place some bamboo skewers in some water to some for at least 1 h 10 min.

2. Get a large mixing bowl: Combine in it all the marinade Ingredients and whisk them well.

3. Cut the chicken thighs into stripes and dip them into the marinade. Cover the bowl with a piece of foil and place it in the fridge for 1 h 30 min.

4. Before you do anything preheat the oven to 375 F.

5. Thread each chicken thigh strip into a bamboo skewer. Lay them on a lined up baking sheet. Cook them in the oven for 32 min.

6. Sprinkle the sesame seeds over the skewers. Serve them warm.

26. Tilapia Fillets

Use fresh tilapia when possible for the most authentic Mongolian flavor!

Prep Time: 5 mins

Total Time: 15 mins

Servings per recipe: 5

Ingredients

- 1 tbsp. oil
- 1/2 tsp garlic, minced
- 5 tilapia fillets
- 1/2 C. brown sugar
- 1/4 C. seasoned rice wine vinegar
- 1/2 C. soy sauce
- 1 tsp fresh ginger, grated

Directions

1. Place a large skillet over medium heat. Add the oil and heat it. Lay in it the tilapia Fillets.

2. Get a mixing bowl: Mix in it the remaining Ingredients to make the sauce. Pour the sauce all over the tilapia. Cook them until the fish is done and sauce is thick.

3. Serve your tilapia fillets with teriyaki sauce warm.

27. Mongolian Beef Meatballs

These meatballs are the beef version of the previously mentioned chicken meatballs but just as delicious!

Prep Time: 10 mins

Total Time: 35 mins

Servings per recipe: 6

Ingredients

- 1 lb. minced beef
- 4 tbsp. teriyaki sauce
- 1/2 tsp grated gingerroot (optional)
- 2 green onions, sliced
- Garlic salt

Directions

1. Preheat oven to 350 F.

2. Get a large mixing bowl: Combine in it all the Ingredients. Combine them well. Shape the mix into 1-inch meatballs.

3. Place meatballs on a lined baking sheet. Then cook them in the oven for 28 min. Serve them warm.

28. Spicy Peanut Butter Dip

Looking for a delicious side dip for your chicken kebobs? Try out this delicious PB recipe!

Prep Time: 5 mins

Total Time: 5 mins

Servings per recipe: 4

Ingredients

- 1/2 C. peanut butter
- 1 tbsp. light soy sauce
- 1 tbsp. chili bean paste
- 2 tsp sugar
- 1/4 C. hot water
- Fresh cilantro

Directions

1. In a bowl, combine peanut butter, soy, chili bean paste, sugar and hot water and beat till well combined.

2. Divide the sauce into 4 small serving bowls and top with the chopped cilantro before serving.

29. Chicken Salad

Quick, simple, and easy to make!

Prep Time: 15 mins

Total Time: 40 mins

Servings per recipe: 4

Ingredients

- 4 C. lettuce, coarsely torn
- 1/2 C. warm water
- 1 tbsp. ginger, minced
- 2 tsp cornstarch
- 1 tbsp. garlic, minced
- 1 tbsp. cold water
- 1/2 lb. chicken tenders, cut into bite size pieces
- 1/2 tsp toasted sesame oil
- 1/2 tsp salt
- 1 tbsp. soy sauce
- 1 tbsp. rice vinegar

Directions

1. In a large skillet, heat oil on medium-high heat and sauté the garlic for about 10 seconds.

2. Add the ginger and sauté till slightly softened.

3. Add the meat and salt cook till browned, breaking the lumps.

4. Stir in the soy sauce, vinegar and warm water and bring to a boil.

5. Combine the cornstarch in the cold water.

6. Add the cornstarch mixture into skillet and stir to combine well.

7. Stir in the sesame oil and remove from the heat.

8. In a wide salad bowl, place the lettuce.

9. Immediately, pour the hot sauce and toss to coat.

10. Serve immediately.

30. Chicken Wontons

Super crispy and delicious, these chicken wontons are an absolute must when making Mongolian food!

Prep Time: 15 mins

Total Time: 25 mins

Servings per recipe: 2

Ingredients

- 8 wonton wrappers
- Sea salt and pepper
- 1/2 lb. ground chicken
- 1 C. Greek yogurt, placed in a cheesecloth-lined sieve (drained overnight in the fridge)
- 1/3 C. onion, minced
- 2 tbsp. fresh parsley, minced
- 4 tsp dried mint
- 1 jalapeño pepper, minced
- 1 tsp garlic, minced

Directions

1. In a bowl, add the lamb, onion, garlic, parsley, jalapeño pepper, salt and black pepper and mix well.

2. Refrigerate to chill completely.

3. Arrange the wrapper onto a smooth surface.

4. Place a tsp of the chicken mixture over each wrapper and fold to form a half circle, sealing with wet fingers.

5. Arrange the dumplings onto baking sheet dusted with the cornstarch.

6. In a pan of the rapidly boiling salted water, add the dumplings and stir once.

7. Cook for about 2 minutes.

8. Transfer onto a paper towels lined plate to drain.

9. In a large sauté pan, add yogurt on medium heat and cook till warmed.

10. Add the hot dumplings and toss to coat well.

11. Divide the dumpling mixture into serving bowls and serve with a sprinkling of the dried mint.

31. Mongolian Style Sauce for Rice and Meats

Prep Time: 15 mins

Total Time: 15 mins

Servings per recipe: 1

Ingredients

- 4 C. hoisin sauce
- 1/2 C. chili oil
- 2 C. plum sauce
- 1 tbsp. sesame oil
- 1 C. oyster sauce
- 1 tbsp. dried orange peel
- 1/2 C. soy sauce
- 2 tbsp. minced garlic
- 1/2 C. Chinese sweet black vinegar
- 3 tbsp. minced ginger
- 1 C. Shaoxing wine
- 1 tbsp. onion powder
- 1/2 C. peanut oil

Directions

1. Combine all Ingredients together.

2. Place in a glass jar and refrigerator overnight before using.

Conclusion

I hope you enjoy these recipes as much as I've enjoyed creating and sharing them with you! Mongolian food is hearty, warm and filling and those are the ideals behind this book. So go ahead, try your hand out at these Mongolian favorites that are guaranteed to please!

About the Author

A native of Indianapolis, Indiana, Valeria Ray found her passion for cooking while she was studying English Literature at Oakland City University. She decided to try a cooking course with her friends and the experience changed her forever. She enrolled at the Art Institute of Indiana which offered extensive courses in the culinary Arts. Once Ray dipped her toe in the cooking world, she never looked back.

When Valeria graduated, she worked in French restaurants in the Indianapolis area until she became the head chef at one of the 5-star establishments in the area. Valeria's attention to taste and visual detail caught the eye of a local business person who expressed an interest in publishing her recipes. Valeria began her secondary career authoring cookbooks and e-books which she tackled with as much talent and gusto as her first career. Her passion for food leaps off the page of her books which have colourful anecdotes and stunning pictures of dishes she has prepared herself.

Valeria Ray lives in Indianapolis with her husband of 15 years, Tom, her daughter, Isobel and their loveable Golden Retriever, Goldy. Valeria enjoys cooking special dishes in her large, comfortable kitchen where the family gets involved in preparing meals. This successful, dynamic chef is an inspiration to culinary students and novice cooks everywhere.

·····•••••••••••••••··

Author's Afterthoughts

Thank you for Purchasing my book and taking the time to read it from front to back. I am always grateful when a reader chooses my work and I hope you enjoyed it!

With the vast selection available online, I am touched that you chose to be purchasing my work and take valuable time out of your life to read it. My hope is that you feel you made the right decision.

I very much would like to know what you thought of the book. Please take the time to write an honest and informative review on Amazon.com. Your experience and opinions will be of great benefit to me and those readers looking to make an informed choice.

With much thanks,

Valeria Ray

CPSIA information can be obtained
at www.ICGtesting.com
Printed in the USA
LVHW091432120521
687223LV00004B/253